laugh.learn.love

For B & C. Happy E!
Love, M.C.

Easter
Volume 4. of the **I spy with my Little Fly** Series

ISBN: **978-1-9995735-8-4**
e-book ISBN: 978-1-9995735-9-1

Text Copyright 2019 By M.C. Goldrick
MotherButterfly Books
Images used in compliance with
Canva's Extended License Agreement
sections 3 e & f, v. 02/2019

All Rights Reserved. No part of this publication may be reproduced or transmitted in any form or by any means, electronic or mechanical, including photocopying, recording, or any information storage and retrieval systems, without permission in writing from the publisher, except for the use of brief quotations in a book review.
Requests for permission to make copies of any part of this work should be submitted online at www.motherbutterfly.com

MotherButterfly
Books

www.motherbutterfly.com

We're small.

We're not noticed at all.

We fly!

We can see from up high.

That's why a fly is a perfect spy.

"Flies care & love to share. We go almost everywhere."

Let's go see:
Easter!

 **LOOK** for hidden flies & bunny eggs. How many you can find?

Find 2 hidden flies & 1 hidden bunny egg.

> Did you hear about the egg who was tickled?

It cracked up!

How do you find the Easter bunny?

Eggs marks the spot!

Find 3 hidden flies & 2 hidden bunny eggs.

The art of painting eggs with wax & dyes started in Ukraine.

Find 5 hidden flies & 2 hidden bunny eggs.

Find 3 hidden flies & 1 hidden bunny egg.

What happened when the Easter Bunny met the rabbit of his dreams?

They lived hoppily ever after!

Easter Lily
Lilium longiflorum

Find 4 hidden flies.

Find 2 hidden bunny eggs.

How do bunnies stay healthy?

Eggercise!

Find 1 hidden flies & 1 hidden bunny egg.

Where does the Easter Bunny get eggs?

From Eggplants!

Find 3 hidden flies & 2 hidden bunny eggs.

Find 3 hidden flies & 2 hidden bunny eggs.

Jump! Twist! Spin!

A Binky:
A jump move bunnies do when they're happy!

Find 2 hidden flies & 1 hidden bunny egg.

What is orange & sounds like a parrot?

A carrot!

Get More Great Reads!
laugh.learn.love

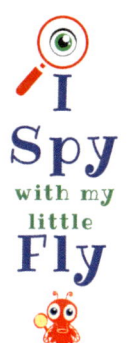

Kitties	Trains	Pizza
Horsies	Planes	Pasta
Pups	Cranes	Cookies
Bears	Boats	Cake
Birdies	Cars	Popcorn
Bunnies	Trucks	Bananas

Visit
www.motherbutterfly.com/giveaway
for books, contests, & more.

   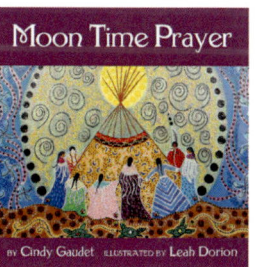

About the Author
M.C. GOLDRICK

Canadian mother of two, M.C. Goldrick lives in Ottawa, Ontario. Born in April, she loves the spring. Easter, and the scent of blossoming lilac bushes, are her favourites!

M.C. loves empathy: the ability to understand & share the feelings of another. Authors need empathy to see the world through different eyes. That's why she loves writing about flies!

Did you know?
Each fly's eye contains 3 to 6 thousand simple eyes!

Loved this Book?

Sharing is Caring!

Please share the love by leaving a review online.

THANK YOU for helping to share our books with families around the world!

- GoodReads
- Amazon
- Indigo
- Barnes and Noble
- iBooks
- Google Play
- Kobo

laugh.learn.love
MotherButterfly.com

Go to
www.motherbutterfly.com/Ispyfun
& get a **FREE** activity book!

Made in the USA
Lexington, KY
16 April 2019